LONDON'S
WEST END BUSES
IN THE 1980s

LONDON'S
WEST END BUSES
IN THE 1980s

VERNON SMITH

AMBERLEY

First published 2019

Amberley Publishing
The Hill, Stroud
Gloucestershire, GL5 4EP

www.amberley-books.com

Copyright © Vernon Smith, 2019

The right of Vernon Smith to be identified as
the Author of this work has been asserted in
accordance with the Copyright, Designs and
Patents Act 1988.

ISBN 978 1 4456 7680 7 (print)
ISBN 978 1 4456 7681 4 (ebook)

British Library Cataloguing in Publication Data.
A catalogue record for this book is available from
the British Library.

Typesetting by Aura Technology and Software
Services, India. Printed in the UK.

Introduction

The West End of London is far more than the two main shopping streets – Oxford Street and Regent Street. It can be regarded to stretch from the City in the east to the River Thames and Marble Arch/Hyde Park/Victoria in the west – the area varies depending on your viewpoint. This area is also home to restaurants, railway stations, theatres, palaces and monuments. Naturally it's also criss-crossed by bus routes and the buses that serve them, bringing people into Central London, moving people from railway stations and taking tourists to the shops and sights.

The eighties will be remembered in the bus world for three things: deregulation, privatisation and bus wars. Deregulation (Transport Act 1985) was the biggest shake up of bus services since the 1930s, abolishing road service licensing, and thus opening routes to competition. The Act also provided for the break-up of the National Bus Company (NBC) and the sale of the various NBC companies. The final part of this was bus wars, when the established operator's most profitable routes came under competition, leading to retaliatory action, and in some cases, gross over-bussing in some towns and cities. Many of the predatory new companies used elderly vehicles, and some were very short-lived. London, as usual, was deemed unsuitable for such goings-on, and a different path would be followed.

London Transport would be broken up (London Regional Transport Act 1984), and the bus operating districts would become eleven quasi-independent companies owned by London Buses Limited until privatised in 1994/5. During 1987 a modified livery with white relief line, grey skirt and a modified roundel started appearing. The bus routes would be put out to tender – usually to the lowest bidder – starting in the suburbs, in 1985, with route 81, which went to London Buslines using older ex-London Transport DMS class buses. Central London would follow with the 24, 176 and 188 soon being operated by Grey-Green, London & Country and Boro'line Maidstone, respectively. Each route lost to a London Buses company meant a shuffle of the newer buses, with the older ones being withdrawn and, in some cases, garages closed.

In this book, we look at various routes and the buses used on them. Not all routes and areas of the West End are covered, but many are. The single

West End garage in Gillingham Street, Victoria, is covered. Opened in 1940, it was unusual, having a basement garage in addition to the street level. It would close in 1993. Victoria was also famous for its covered bus station – a draughty place with the narrowest pavements going, buses roared past with inches to spare! In the eighties crew operation was still common, as was the Routemaster, but the routes themselves were very different from the routes we know today. Using route 1 as an example, you could travel from Aldwych to Bromley, Kent, on a single bus. On today's shortened routes, it takes three different buses on three different routes. Many well-known routes are covered, in addition to the various vehicle types. Also covered are non-London buses and selected sightseeing buses of the time.

This book mainly features my own photographs, with help from a selection of other photographers. Any mistakes are purely my own, and if I have not credited an image correctly, please accept my apologies and let me know. Two very useful websites used during the compiling of this book were Ian's Bus Stop (http://countrybus.org) and London Bus Routes (https://www.londonbuses.co.uk) by Ian Armstrong.

Bromley Common's (TB) T282 starts the long journey from Aldwych to Bromley on route 1. Although painted in the new colours, it still looks down-at-heel. T282 would finish service with Stagecoach Devon in 1997.

Also on the 1, TB have put out LS216. Time was running out for this long route, being cut back to Surrey Quays Station in 1991. Route 1 currently runs between Tottenham Court Road Station and Canada Water.

New Cross' RM1261 is leaving Whitehall, while on diversion from its normal route, via the Strand. In this May 1987 view, route 1 went all the way to Marylebone Station.

Seen loading in Victoria is L157, ready to head to West Norwood. Route 2 would be withdrawn in 1992, to be partly replaced by the 322. L157 would be withdrawn by Arriva North East in 2004.

Still in Victoria is Norwood's (N) RM2217 on the 2B to Crystal Palace. Upon later conversion to OPO, the route became plain 2. Note the painted over via point, top left.

Camberwell's (Q) RML2273 passes through Trafalgar Square on its way to Crystal Palace. The 3 was running between there and Oxford Circus, having been cut back from Camden Town in 1987.

Another Camberwell bus, RM837 passes the Houses of Parliament in April 1988. Route 3 still reaches Crystal Palace, now using New Routemasters.

Nearing journey's end, M1067 passes St Clement Danes Church before turning left onto Waterloo Bridge in March 1988. Route 4 still connects Archway and Waterloo.

Heading to Archway, M1076 (from London Northern's Holloway Garage) sweeps around Aldwych in May 1989. New in 1984, M1076 would pass to Ensign in 2005.

Leaving Theobalds Road is T195 making for Waterloo. The current route 5 goes nowhere near Waterloo but does get to Romford. T195 would finish its service days on Merseyside.

Wearing an interesting mix of fresh lower deck paint, and a very faded, damaged roof, is Ash Grove's RML884 in this June 1988 shot. RML884 would last to the end of RML operation in 2005 before disposal to Ensign.

In an equally patchy livery is RML2726, complete with tourist adverts and yellow blinds/relief band. The 6 ran from Kensal Rise to Hackney Wick, but now it just connects Willesden and Aldwych.

Fresh from the paint shop is RML2356, crossing the junction of Strand and Waterloo Bridge, in March 1988. After withdrawal in 2005, this bus was exported to Guadeloupe.

Standing at Bloomsbury, Red Lion Square, is RM2094 of Westbourne Park. The painters had done the lower deck only, leaving a scruffy looking vehicle.

Held up by a protest, RML885, freshly painted, is in a line of parked buses in New Oxford Street in July 1990. The route has since been cut back to terminate at Oxford Circus.

Passing Tottenham Court Road Station is RM2031, leading an RML along the New Oxford Street bus lane in April 1988. RM2031 was withdrawn the following year.

Bow's RML2695 heads to Bow Church. The route still links Bow and the West End, but no longer goes to Willesden, now turning at Tottenham Court Road.

Laying over beside St Mary le Strand Church, Strand, is RML2739, taking a break from the 9. New in 1967, it would last in service until 2004, when it was sold to Ensign.

In June 1987 RM1555 is heading for Liverpool Street Station – a destination no longer served by the modern day 9, all buses turning at Aldwych.

Heading along Bloomsbury Street is RML2511, bound for Hammersmith. The current route 10 still runs between Kings Cross and Hammersmith, using New Routemasters.

Ash Grove's RML2534 is on the stand at Trafalgar Square in June 1983. This part of Trafalgar Square is now one way in the opposite direction. RML2534 would be exported to Nova Scotia in 2009.

Seen leaving Whitehall again is RML2534, displaying its tourist advertising for the 11 in May 1987. Today's route 11 still heads to Liverpool Street Station.

Crossing Parliament Square is RM1946, en route to Chelsea Worlds End, during May 1988. New in 1964, withdrawal came at the end of 1993.

Gillingham Street (GM) had two RMs in General livery. Passing around Aldwych in 1989, RM1590 makes for Liverpool Street Station. It would finish its days in a variety of non-PSV roles.

Caught in Trafalgar Square is GM's RM89, also working the 11 to Liverpool Street Station. RM89 would be exported to Argentina in 1998.

Loading in Victoria is GM's RM1188 in July 1990. This bus was withdrawn and scrapped in 1993.

RML2499 is seen in 1990 heading for Dulwich. The 12 was one of the routes operated by Mercedes 'bendy buses' for just over five years.

Camberwell's RM1018 makes its way across Trafalgar Square on its way to Dulwich, Plough. The modern-day 12 still links Oxford Circus and Dulwich.

Broken down in Trafalgar Square is Finchley's RML2478, seen in April 1987. The 13 now connects Victoria with North Finchley.

Not in the best condition is RM1986. Despite its Selkent district sticker, it's working from Finchley in this 1985 view and looks in need of a paintbrush.

Caught outside of Charing Cross Station, in far better condition, is RML2569, complete with tourist posters either side of the destination. (M. J. Beckham)

Resting on the stand in Aldwych in February 1988 is Finchley's RML2727. In 1993 the route was lost on tendering to BTS, who used Routemasters in their own route branded livery.

Finchley kept an immaculate showbus, RML903, complete with advertising for bus hire. It is seen in Aldwych in April 1988.

An unusual case of a Metrobus in crew mode on the 13, with a conductor. M443 is seen crossing Trafalgar Square in July 1987. Converted to part open top in 2008, it would be scrapped in 2010.

Tottenham Court Road Station is the setting for Putney's RML2745, resting between turns on the 14 in April 1989. This bus was sold to Ensign in 2003.

In May 1989, RML2316 races along Bloomsbury Street, making for Putney Heath Green Man. Withdrawn in 2005, it was another Routemaster exported to Canada.

Bloomsbury Street again. RML2343, with yellow tourist relief band, is heading for Fulham. RML2343 would move to Edinburgh for Ghost Bus Tours.

London Northern had a handful of second-hand Metrobuses. M1482 (VRG 416T) was an ex-Tyne & Wear example. Sold to Merseybus in 1993, it would go on to work for City Sightseeing.

The 14A was a partial replacement for the northern section of the 14. M1483, another ex-Tyne & Wear Metrobus, nears journey's end. M1483 would follow M1482 to Merseybus and City Sightseeing.

More common on the 14A, standard Metrobus M1217 is on the stand at Tottenham Court Road Station in April 1988. Withdrawn in 2000, it would go on to work for Halifax Joint Committee.

London Coaches LC1, one of a pair of Olympian/East Lancs seventy seaters, was originally used on London Liner services between London and Eastbourne, but is now used for contracts and private hires.

Parked beside St Mary le Strand is sister vehicle LC2, seen in April 1988. Two years later both LC class coaches were sold to Southampton City Transport.

Another London Coaches vehicle, LS76, working for the Japanese School. This bus has high-backed seats and had been converted to single door, originally for the X99 Forester service.

The training fleet was made up of Routemasters and DMS's in the eighties. Seen in August 1989 is Selkent's RM1970, which left London service in 2004.

With a primer painted blind box, RML2740 heads around Aldwych to Upton Park in April 1988. RML274 would be withdrawn from Westbourne Park in 2004.

Crossing Trafalgar Square is Upton Park's RML2309, making for Ladbroke Grove. Today's 15 runs between Blackwall and Trafalgar Square. Withdrawn in 2004, it was exported to Nova Scotia in 2009.

Ready to return to East Ham on the 15B is another Upton Park bus, RML2581. In 2004 this bus was exported to Poland.

Express route X15 used both RMA and RMC Routemasters. Here RMC1485 heads back to East Becton. Currently RMC1485 is owned by Ensign.

Another express route was the X1, operated by Reading Transport, linking the West End with Reading. Olympian 84 crosses Trafalgar Square.

Reading Transport Metrobus 143 is also seen in Trafalgar Square. After downgrading to bus status A143 AMO would pass to Ruffle Coaches, Halstead, Essex.

RML2384 has been struck from behind by RM1101, outside Holborn Underground Station. Despite the location, traffic moves easily past the scene.

Inspectors take down the details of the incident. Note the small amount of damage and the lack of hi-vis jackets! After a spell with the Wirral Transport Museum, RM1101 is currently with Ghost Bus Tours, York.

RML2384 had been moved out of the way, giving us the chance to see the damage to its rear offside. RML2384 was last used as living accommodation by a County Durham inn.

Passing Red Lion Square on the 19 in June 1987, RML2310 is still showing where its former tourist posters had been removed. Another 2004 withdrawal, it's still in use with Timebus.

Holloway's RM88 leads the queue of buses in the New Oxford Street bus lane on a dull April day in 1988. Withdrawn at the end of the year, it was exported to Germany in 1990.

Passing Red Lion Square, RM599 makes for Clapham Junction in May 1989. Route 19 was famous for having Kentish Bus-liveried RMLs from 1993.

At the same location is M1115. The current-day 19 runs between Finsbury Park and Battersea Bridge and is operated by London General. M1115 was withdrawn by Metroline in 2001.

Found attending an RML breakdown on New Oxford Street is LS454, now in use as a mobility bus at Ash Grove. LS454 would go on to operate with Capital Citybus and First PMT.

Grey-Green had several double-deck coaches for use on their commuter routes. Here, B102XYH, a Plaxton 4000, passes Bedford Square.

Passing Trafalgar Square is a Scania K90, with East Lancs body, E108 JYV. Grey-Green would later downgrade this to a normal service bus.

Seen on the Red Lion Square stand is RML2410, with the conductor chatting to the driver. In 1993, this would become one of the Kentish Bus-liveried RMLs.

Arriving at Trafalgar Square in February 1989 on the 22B is T376, one of many Titans to be sold to Merseybus in the nineties.

Homerton-bound T53 is seen in May 1988. T53 was sold to Ensign in 1994, before onward sale to Kinch, Barrow upon Soar.

Seen on driver familiarisation in January 1990 is Kentish Bus Atlantean 624, in advance of Kentish Bus taking over the 22A/B and 55 in January and February 1990.

Working from a base in Leyton, Kentish Bus ordered forty-three Leyland Olympians with Northern Counties two-door bodies. Here 550 has turned short in New Oxford Street.

Passing Red Lion Square on the 22B is Olympian 545 when only two months old. 545 would finish its days as a school bus with Arriva North East in 2011.

Resting at Trafalgar Square is Chalk Farm's RML2262, a bus that would be sold by Ensign to a funeral service for use as a double-deck hearse.

The 24 was converted to OPO Titan operation in October 1986. After London, T474 went on to spend five years with South Coast Buses (Stagecoach) at Hastings.

Titan T518 crosses Parliament Square in April 1988. By the year's end, the 24 would be awarded to Grey-Green using brand new Volvos.

Upon winning the 24, Grey-Green ordered thirty Volvo Citybuses with Alexander bodies, all of which were ready for the 5 November start date. Seen in 1989 is 132 heading for Pimlico.

Bow's RM1138 is seen Victoria bound on the 25. The tourist posters have no route number, so buses on the 8, which served some of the same points, could still use them.

Another of Bow's Routemasters, RM1150 makes tracks for Ilford in this August 1987 view. In late 1988 this bus was exported to Sri Lanka.

Route 25 converted to OPO Titan operation in January 1988 as shown by Bow's T558 in July 1989. T558 would end its days with Stagecoach United Counties around 2004.

Swinging into New Oxford Street in May 1988 is RM2190 on the 29 to Victoria. RM2190 would be withdrawn the following year.

Flying across Trafalgar Square is RM385, again making for Victoria. After refurbishment it would survive in London until 2004. It is now with London Retro Bus Hire.

Further along the route RM632 crosses Parliament Square in May 1988. Withdrawn in November of the same year, it was later exported to Japan.

Seen working as a crew bus, M613 is on the stand in Trafalgar Square in June 1983. M613 would later serve in Liverpool with Glenvale Transport.

RM1005 is seen at Brockley waiting to start its journey on the 36A to Victoria. Re-registered ALC 290A from 5 CLT in January 1991, it would see refurbishment, finally finishing London service in 2005. Now owned by Peter Hendy, it still sees regular use. (M. J. Beckham)

Not my best picture, but it shows a Peckham RM2159 on the 36B heading along the Strand on diversion – note the police motor bike in this June 1983 shot.

Seen in Victoria in April 1988 is re-registered RM9. Originally VLT9, it was registered OYM 374A whilst at Peckham, regaining VLT9 in 1995. Adopted by New Cross as a showbus, it is still used for special events by Go Ahead London.

Receipt of Purchase

Invicta Model Rail Ltd

Invicta Till 1
www.Invictamodelrail.com
130 Station Rd Sidcup Kent 0208 302 7774

Items:

Product	Price	Qty	Total
Misc Magazines		1	£13.50

Total Qty: 1

Sub Total:	£13.50
Date:	23/12/2019 13:07:08
Staff:	Manager
Device:	Till1
Total:	£13.50

Tenders

Card:	£13.50
- Change:	£0.00

Please retain your receipt for refunds within 14
days from the date of purchase

Thank you for shopping with Invicta
www.invictamodelrail.com

RECB00009SN103H30960

Seen leaving Proctor Street in September 1986 is RML2368, displaying tourist posters used by route 38 and 55 buses. RML2368 was withdrawn in 2004.

When the posters only applied to the 38, route numbers appeared to the left of the blinds. RML2384 is seen in a spot of trouble on the New Oxford Street stand.

On the same stand but using Bloomsbury as its ultimate destination is Leyton showbus RM1676. In 1999 this bus was exported to Canada to work with Double Deck Tours.

In the late 1980s/90s many crew routes became OPO on Sunday. On a sunny Sunday in October 1988, T452 makes its way to Victoria.

In the days when Victoria Bus Station was covered and had very narrow stands between the buses, RML2334 looks fresh after a repaint in this April 1988 view.

The crew of New Cross RM582 enjoy a chat after terminating at Charing Cross/Trafalgar Square in June 1983. It would be withdrawn and scrapped two years later.

The 53 terminated in the south-east at Plumstead Common, but Plumstead Garage journeys were extended to Plumstead Station. A scruffy RM613 is outside the garage in May 1987.

The 53 converted to OPO in 1988, after which both Titans and L class Olympians could be seen on the route. In April 1988 T839 makes the turn into Whitehall.

Plumstead's L123 makes the same right turn, while running with its front doors open in May 1988. L123 would transfer to Stagecoach East Scotland, before withdrawal in 2007.

Heading back to South London through Trafalgar Square is L20, which lasted in London service until 2004. The 53 only runs from Plumstead to Whitehall currently.

On the Tottenham Court Road Station stand is RML2368, displaying point of interest posters for routes 38 and 55.

Titan T333 leaves Bloomsbury in 1987 and shows the now OPO version of the 55. Bought by Merseybus in 1994, it was withdrawn by Arriva North West in 2004.

London Buses lost the 55 to Kentish Bus, who obtained new Olympians with two-door Northern Counties bodywork in March 1990. 519 makes for Tottenham Court Road Station.

Kentish Bus 555 clearly shows its dual doors and split-level front step in April 1990, when only a month old. It was used as a training vehicle from 2003 until sale in 2005.

Although a little outside our area, T1068 looks great under Holborn Viaduct while on the 63 to Peckham.

Trunk route 68 ploughed from Euston to South Croydon daily. Rounding Aldwych on 21 August 1988 is Croydon's DM2637.

Metrobuses were also to be seen on the 68. Early M214 loads for West Croydon in the Strand during 1990.

Also found on the 68 were the L-Class Olympians. L24 crosses Waterloo Bridge bound for South Croydon Garage in June 1988. LS24 would be sold in 2006 to Truronian, Truro, Cornwall.

Still in as-delivered red, Olympian L183 leaves the Aldwych stop in the nineties. Sold to Ensign in 2004, it would become an open-top sightseeing bus.

Victoria Bus Station, with RML2372 demonstrating just how narrow the stands were while awaiting departure for Tottenham Swan. Note yet another style of route branding. (M. J. Beckham)

Parked in Gillingham Street's (GM-Victoria) side yard in June 1983 is New Cross's DMS1997, ready to return on the 70 to Surrey Docks Station.

At the same location in 1983 is DMS1668, surviving until the end of 1983. It is also displaying the ultimate blind for the 188 to Euston, as opposed to the route it's on – the 70.

Filling Victoria's front doors are M1364 and RM1357. The 52 is displaying yet another route promotion idea used in 1987!

It's April 1988 and found in this doorway were RM593 and M865. Opened in 1940, it would close in 1993 before being demolished in 1999.

In 1983, the side yard of GM had RM2207 parked between duties on the 2B. At the end of 1988 the bus was exported to Sri Lanka.

Found inside the maintenance bays were RM1725 and B20 DMS driver trainer DM2454. The DM would become an open topper with Big Bus Co. in 1994. (M. J. Beckham)

Parked inside the Victoria's main shed is RM1125, which has been re-registered KGH 858A. It would last until 2004, when it was withdrawn from Brixton. (M. J. Beckham)

Training bus RMC1508 leads a line of National Express and Armstrong Galley vehicles undergoing servicing and layover at GM in April 1988.

In 1987 one of the doorways is filled by Metrobus M856 and RM873, complete with yellow tourist relief band. M856 would be exported to France in 2000.

Inside GM, in June 1983, was a line of gleaming RMs, all blinded for the 2B and led by RM279. Red Arrow LS472 peeks in behind!

Tucked in by Sightseeing B20 DMS's and Red Arrow Leyland National 2s was former SMD441, then in use as a London Transport Recruitment vehicle. It is seen on 12 June 1983.

With LS472 on the left, this June 1983 shows a line of six RMs (led by RM279), with an LS, another RM, and a B20 DMS filling the picture.

In use by the Transport & General Workers Union was DMS806 (new in 1984), seen in the garage in June 1988.

Parked, in 1989, on the ramp that led to the garage's basement is sightseeing coach TOH 745S. The basement would see further use as a minibus base.

Parked up around the corner from the garage is Eastern National KOO 790V, fully blinded up for the long 402 to Southend Central Bus Station.

Passing Bedford Square in 1988 on the 73, bound for Palace Gate, Kensington, is Tottenham's RML2611. Withdrawn in 2004, it was exported to Eire in 2017.

Further down Bloomsbury Street a gaggle of buses, led by RML2346, sprint from the traffic lights.

Picking up at Holborn Station in 1990 is DMS1890, heading to Euston on the 77. Note the painted over side blinds and both styles of roundel.

April 1987 sees Stockwell's DMS2269 loading in Aldwych before heading to Clapham Junction on the 77A. DMS2269 was withdrawn in 1991.

At journey's end of the 82 is M482 in July 1990. New in December 1980, Metroline would withdraw it in 2001.

Heading across Trafalgar Square is Stockwell Garage's RML2576, making for Tooting, Mitre. RML2576 would stay in London until 2005 before export to Germany.

An immaculate RML2680 heads across Parliament Square in April 1988 whilst working the 88 to Tooting. This bus lasted until 2005, before sale to Ensign.

RM264 heads for its stand in Trafalgar Square, with two more Routemasters and a Titan in hot pursuit.

Starting the long journey to Southend is Southend Transport's 703 (UPE 204M), an ex-London Country Leyland National.

Delivered new to Southend Transport. Leopard/Duple BTE205V passes Trafalgar Square in May 1990.

Sister coach BTE 208V has minor livery differences compared to BTE205V. It has been caught in Trafalgar Square at the start of its long drive to Southend.

Southend 502 YHB 20T makes for Southend.

Used on the X1 and Culturebus tours were six Cardiff bus Olympians that Southend hired from 1986–88. B559 ATX passes Bedford Square on a lightly used 614 tour.

London Transport bought as many London Country Routemasters as it could, using many still in their old liveries as training buses. RMC1499 is seen in June of 1983.

The driver of London Coaches E604 LVH keeps a watchful eye on the taxi cab at his rear while negotiating Trafalgar Square in 1990.

Brixton's M1088 takes a break from the 109 in June 1988. Transferred to Arriva North East in 2000, it would last another two years before sale to Ensign and scrapping.

Also seen in 1988 is M1440, which Brixton had adopted as a garage 'pet', being the last standard (not second-hand) Metrobus delivered to LT. This bus would later be painted in General livery.

Turning into Whitehall is Thornton Heath's B20 DMS2316, looking slightly worse for wear. DMS2316 would be withdrawn in 1991.

Picking up passengers on the 134, for the two stops to Tottenham Court Road Station, is Muswell Hill's T802, which finished its service life with Stagecoach Bluebird.

Seen at Warren Street, RM804 heads for Marble Arch on the 135, a route only crew operated for one year, from 1987 to 1988. RM804 would be re-registered MFF 581 and sold shortly afterwards in 1994.

Pulling away from the stand on John Princes Street, on the long journey to Crystal Palace, is Brixton's RML2573. The 137 now turns at Streatham Hill. (M. J. Beckham)

Seen underneath Holborn Viaduct in July 1989 is T712. Route 141 no longer runs south to Catford, now travelling between Palmers Green and London Bridge. This bus would be exported to the USA in 2010.

Seen at Waterloo before returning to Enfield is M676. The 149 no longer serves Waterloo, London Bridge now being the terminal point. M676 would finish its service life with Glenvale, Merseyside.

Clearly fresh from repaint in 1989 is RM348, crossing Trafalgar Square on its way to Streatham on the 159. This bus was re-registered in 2004 to 851 UXC.

On a short to Kennington Church is RML2469, on a sunny day in May 1990. Sold to Ensign in 2004, the bus became part of Ensign's Routemaster Raffle.

Camberwell's RM199 passes Trafalgar Square on the 159, which became the last of London's crew routes eighteen years later in 2005. RM199 was scrapped in 1988.

Introduced to replace parts of the 68 in 1986, the 168 converted from Titans to Leyland Nationals in 1989, as shown by LS384, which, like many of its kind, was withdrawn in 1990.

Chalk Farm Garage have LS388 on the 168, seen in Russell Square in 1990. LS388 was withdrawn later in the same year. Route 168 was lost to Grey-Green in September 1990.

LS258 rounds Aldwych in January 1990. This bus was withdrawn only six months later, when twelve years old.

In 1987, Titans still ruled the 168, as seen by Chalk Farm's T628, in the Aldwych. Chalk Farm Garage would close late in 1992, and T628 would finish life with Stagecoach Merseyside.

One of the experimental buses, M1442, is seen in Aldwych. Part of vehicle trials involving Dennis Dominators, Volvo Ailsas and Leyland Olympians, the successful bus was the Olympian.

Another of Stockwell's experimentals, Dominator H1 is seen in 1985. The Dominators would later join the London Coaches fleet, H1 being withdrawn in 1992.

Seen leaving Kingsway is tourist yellow banded T997. Originally intended for the 188, the idea was quickly dropped so the buses could be used on all of New Cross' OPO routes. T997 became a dining bus in 2004.

New Cross' T915 makes for Forest Hill on the 171. Although slightly shortened at its northern end, the southern end was extended to Catford Bus Garage.

Introduced in 1986 between Waterloo and Tottenham, this route currently runs between County Hall and Northumberland Park. Here we see M1152 approaching Waterloo in 1989.

Not long before the withdrawal of the original route 172, in 1985, Camberwell's RM250 crosses Kingsway bound for Kings Cross.

A smart T989 makes its way to Camberwell Green in June 1989. The 176 currently runs between Tottenham Court Road Station and Penge.

Camberwell's T760 heads for Forest Hill on the 176 during 1988. Route 176 would be won by London & Country in 1990. T760 would finish its days on Merseyside.

Won by London & Country in November 1990, various types of vehicles were used on the 176, pending delivery of new Volvos. Here indigenous AN173 helps out.

Atlanteans were also hired from South Yorkshire. Here Mainline-liveried 1726 picks up in the Strand, complete with correct blind displays.

Also in the Strand is South Yorkshire-liveried 1764. All of the hired buses featured full blind displays.

Volvo/Northern Counties 641 also takes a turn on the 176, but with only a route number showing (no destination blinds). After life with L&C, it went onto work with Arriva Kent & Sussex, Medway Towns and West Sussex, before sale to Ensign.

Seen in the Strand, new Volvo Citybus 679 collects passengers on its way to Penge in January 1991. 679 would go on to work for Arriva The Shires, Manchester, Merseyside, and other independents before scrapping in 2014.

Heading across Waterloo Bridge for Euston is New Cross' DMS1668, which would be withdrawn at the end of 1983.

New Cross Titan T1064 makes for Greenwich in May 1988. The 188 would be won by Boro'line Maidstone in November 1988.

While awaiting new vehicles, Boro'line hired buses from Ipswich and Nottingham. Passing Russell Square in December 1989 is Nottingham Fleetline 200.

Ipswich Atlantean No. 1 is seen at the same location, complete with limited route branding for the 188 under the lower-deck windows.

Boro'line would even put their ex-Tayside Ailsa's out on the 188, as shown by 911 in February 1989. Note the lack of destination details.

The new Volvo Citybuses with Alexander bodywork had arrived by June 1989. Boro'line's 921 is seen cruising through Aldwych.

The arrival of new buses on the 188 didn't stop Boro'line using any vehicle. Here is ex-London Buses LS436 loading in the Strand in December 1990.

Route 239 received new Mercedes/Alexander minibuses under the Streetline brand. MA120 reaches journey's end in summer 1990, not long after introduction on the 239.

Route 400, the Armada Express, ran between Central London and Greenwich and the Thames Barrier. Selkent Travel's L260 heads for Embankment in August 1988.

The following year, the 400 returned, with the Selkent Olympians carrying Bountybus branding, as shown by L262, leaning into the right-hand turn for Embankment.

Leyland National Mk 2 LS501 passes Red Lion Square on Red Arrow 501 in May 1989. This bus was converted into a National Greenway in 1993.

LS455 has had its roundel moved to the rear to make space for an advertising frame when seen in Aldwych on the 502 in 1988. Also converted to a Greenway in 1994.

In November 1988, unbranded and scruffy looking LS464 is parked up at Waterloo, Cornwall Road. Route 503 only lasted three years before being withdrawn.

Freshly repainted but lacking its Red Arrow branding, a gleaming LS442 passes around Aldwych in June 1988. Converted to a Greenway in 1993, it was scrapped in 2007.

Showing the new Red Arrow livery, LS446 is seen on the 509 in May 1989 – a route that would only operate for two years before withdrawal in October 1989.

An overall view of the Cornwall Street, Waterloo, Red Arrow base in 1991, with a solitary Metrobus amongst the Leyland Nationals.

Airbus M1013 joins Proctor Street in July 1988, showing off its original-style branding. Downgraded to normal seating and single doored, withdrawal would follow in 2002.

Showing its new style Airbus branding, M1008 passes through Russell Square. M1008 was also downgraded to normal seating and single doored in 2000.

Hired by London Transport, and used on the C1, was Manchester's Little Gem E216 WVM – seen in Victoria.

More normal vehicles on the C1 were Optare Citypacers; OV9 is seen in Victoria. Most Citypacers would have short lives, being withdrawn in 1991–92.

After a duty on the N19, Victoria's M1354 is seen parked beside its home garage in 1990. M1354 would transfer to Arriva Northumbria in 2000, being withdrawn in 2007.

Working tourist route Z1, which linked Baker Street and London Zoo, is M1151, a bus that would be sold to Ensign in 2003, before scrapping in 2007.